P9-CFP-837

Most Schools Won't Fit

Most Schools Won't Fit

EVERY PARENT'S DILEMMA
AND WHAT TO DO ABOUT IT

• • •

Don Berg and Holly Allen

© 2017 Don Berg and Holly Allen
All rights reserved.

ISBN: 1546974458
ISBN 13: 9781546974451

Contents

Preface

• • •

THIS IS THE STORY OF a wrong idea.

In particular, it's the story of how our school system, under the influence of that wrong idea, does harm. Despite the fact that experts in at least two fields—psychology and education—overwhelmingly recognize it as false, its influence has steadily grown in the last fifty years. Intuitively compelling and simple to implement, it guides educational policy in ways that sound reasonable on paper but utterly fail in practice.

The idea is about how people learn; we call it the "delivery model." The famous education activist and scholar Paulo Freire called it the "banking model." Other scholars and commentators have other names for it. The core idea is that one person can take knowledge out of his own brain and stuff it into someone else's.

Coauthors Don Berg and Holly Allen approach the delivery method from different perspectives. Berg has come to understand the delivery model and its effects after more than two decades of working with children in self-directed educational systems and studying psychology. He is one of only a few researchers who have studied the motivational patterns of students in nonmainstream settings.

For Allen, the importance of the delivery model is immediate and personal—she has three young children. Drawing on her own educational experiences, degrees in biochemistry and computer science, and her experience as a parent, she's been searching for how best to help her children succeed in the world without running afoul of the downsides of mainstream education.

This book will not explain how to fix our school system. What it will do is give you an understanding of how and why the school system can inadvertently do as much harm as good to a child, and how you can protect the children you care about.

CHAPTER 1

The Epidemic

• • •

AT NO TIME IN HISTORY have we better understood how our own minds work or how learning occurs; yet almost none of that understanding has impacted our education system, public or private.

This is, on the face of it, a fantastic claim. We tend to assume that greater understanding leads almost automatically to better systems. Once we figured out how to build houses, it no longer made sense to live in caves. Once we figured out that germs cause contagious diseases, it no longer made sense to bleed people to "balance their humors" (and too often kill them,[1] as happened to George Washington). Once we figured out how to build electronic computers, it no longer made sense to employ armies of people to make manual calculations.[2]

Anyone with even a little knowledge of schooling over the past century might also be forgiven for being skeptical of such a claim. After all, haven't there been countless waves of reform in that time—new methods of teaching math, reading, spelling, and history? What about open classrooms, project-based learning, and jigsaw classrooms? What about recent technological innovations, such as electronic whiteboards and the One Laptop-per-Child initiative?

---

1 The switch from the miasma theory, which called for "balancing humors," to the germ theory is described in both Steven Johnson's book, *The Ghost Map*, and in medical historian, David Wootton's book, *Bad Medicine*.

2 The "based on a true story" and Academy Award-nominated movie, *Hidden Figures*, tells the story of how the term "computers" at NASA changed its reference point from women to electronic equipment during the sixties space race.

But all the reforms and innovations that have been so ardently pursued in schools have been about as meaningful as nineteenth-century physicians arguing over which particular vein to pierce and how much blood to let flow.

Here's why.

The Familiar Problem

First, let's revisit the problem. Chances are that if you're reading this, you're aware that the American school system is considered to be in a crisis that threatens to destroy our national prosperity and way of life. Our test scores—the measurements on which our society depends more and more heavily as an indicator of success—remain consistently mediocre despite ever more desperate reforms. Of more immediate impact is that the students who graduate from our high schools are routinely found to be ill prepared for either college or the workforce, and employers are no more enthusiastic about those graduating from college.[3] Even if we simply want to prepare people for the workforce, we are not doing a very good job.

If you have higher aspirations for education—for example, that it might help people fulfill their own potential, learn to think well, or become good citizens—you are likely to be even more disappointed.

This problem is not new. In the last two centuries, school has become a nearly universal part of childhood throughout the world. At this point, children in this country spend more than half of their waking hours in it. We have a deeply vested interest in anything that impacts our children, and with the weight on school to provide our kids with all the skills and knowledge they need to prosper in the world, it's no wonder we focus so much attention on it. For years, decades—arguably centuries—people have been talking about how to fix the school system.

Most of the proposed fixes, even those proposed a century ago, sound familiar. New methods of presenting material are always popular and always

---

3 Berr, J. (2016). Employers: New College Grads Aren't Ready for Workplace. *CBS News Money Watch*. Retrieved from http://www.cbsnews.com/news/employers-new-college-grads-arent-ready-for-workplace

hotly contested. (Try livening up the conversation among a group of parents by throwing out the phrase "whole language versus phonics.") As testing has become more influential, proposals to test more often and more rigorously have gained support. Push people harder, and they'll perform better, right? At the same time, interestingly, material is often simplified to remove any nuance or ambiguity that might cause a child to stumble. And money is always a heated topic. Even adjusted for inflation, we spend more than twice as much per student now as we did fifty years ago.[4] In fact, we spend more per student than most countries in the world, including those that consistently score higher than we do on standardized tests.

Then there's the push for teacher accountability. The teachers are the ones who are supposed to be doing the actual work in these crucial school settings; they're responsible for making certain that each child reaches his or her potential. So why not focus on measuring (and incentivizing) teacher effectiveness, so that we can reward good teachers and weed out the bad ones?

Looking back on even just the recent decades of school reform, surveying the dizzying array of programs aimed at improving education, it's easy to feel a bit overwhelmed—"No Child Left Behind," "Race to the Top," and the "Every Student Succeeds Act" are the names of just the central federal programs since 2001. And inevitably, if one can withdraw from the morass for a few minutes and take a step back, another question arises: why hasn't any of this worked? Or, when success is declared, why are the improvements so small?

Despite all the ideas and work and restructuring, things aren't improving. In some ways, things seem to be getting worse. The usual culprits are lined up: we still aren't using the right methods of teaching; we don't offer students the right incentives to perform; we don't invest enough money in our educational system; and we can't get rid of the "bad" teachers.

---

4 U.S. Department of Education. (2005). *10 Facts about K-12 Education Funding*. Washington, DC: Author. Retrieved from https://www2.ed.gov/about/overview/fed/10facts/index.html

But the truth is that all these reforms are working around the edges of the central issue, one that goes unrecognized by the majority of parents, media, and policy makers. There is a fundamental problem in our approach to education, a problem that undermines all the good intentions of the many talented and passionate people involved.

And we can begin to grasp the problem by considering its most direct and pervasive symptom: disengagement.

THE EPIDEMIC

Disengagement gets an occasional mention in discussions about school, but only as a side issue. It has long been recognized that students typically start school with all the excitement that characterizes being six years old, and somewhere along the way their enthusiasm diminishes. And this isn't just an informal observation—for more than thirty years, patterns of motivation in mainstream schools have been studied repeatedly. Using a variety of theoretical and methodological approaches, all studies of mainstream schools—public, private, and charter—have observed the same effect: statistically, student engagement declines throughout the entire span of compulsory schooling.[5] The phenomenon is so widespread that many people accept it as inevitable.

---

5 References regarding declines in engagement and intrinsic motivation:
  Bouffard, T., Marcoux, M., Vezeau, C., & Bordeleau, L. (2003). Changes in self- perceptions of competence and intrinsic motivation among elementary school children. *British Journal of Educational Psychology*, 73, 171–186.
  Corpus, J. H., McClintic-Gilbert, M. S., & Hayenga, A. O. (2009). Within-year changes in children's intrinsic and extrinsic motivational orientations: Contextual predictors and academic outcomes. *Contemporary Educational Psychology*, 34, 154–166. DOI: 10.1016/j.cedpsych.2009.01.001
  Gottfried, A. E., Fleming, J. S., & Gottfried, A. W. (2001). Continuity of academic intrinsic motivation from childhood through late adolescence: A longitudinal study. *Journal of Educational Psychology*, 93, 3–13. DOI: 10.1037/0022-0663.93.1.3
  Harter, S. (1981). A new self-report scale of intrinsic versus extrinsic orientation in the classroom: Motivational and informational components. *Developmental Psychology*, 17, 300–312. DOI: 10.1037/0012-1649.17.3.300
  Hunter, J. P., & Csikszentmihalyi, M. (2003). The positive psychology of interested adolescents. *Journal of Youth and Adolescence*, 32, 27–35. DOI: 10.1023/A:1021028306392

What does disengagement look like? In students, there are three main symptoms such as the following:

* Some students simply drop out. This is the simplest and most obvious form of disengagement. Dropping out is usually preceded by the student tuning out, often years earlier.
* Some students remain in school but fail to perform. Underachievement can have a variety of faces—there seems to be a vast difference between a student who consistently tries, yet struggles, and one who rejects his or her schooling—but the net effect is similar.
* But there's a third, less recognized symptom: "fauxchievement." Fauxchievement is when a student does the required work to achieve whatever minimal grade he or she finds acceptable but fails to actually engage with the material. The student is playing the game, jumping through the hoops, but emotionally he or she has checked out.

This last symptom may seem harmless—in fact, doesn't everyone do that? But there's a long-term consequence to faking one's way through school. Studies on adults found that at least half of all college-degree holders managed to get their degrees without fundamentally understanding basic principles.[6] This means that they are unable to solve the most basic problems in their field of specialization when those problems are presented in a real-world manner, rather than how it would have been presented on a school test. In other words, they've jumped through all the right hoops but have failed to really master the concepts.

Think about that. How would you feel knowing that your brain surgeon failed to grasp basic medical concepts? The evidence cited earlier implies that this is actually true of at least half of all doctors.

Lepper, M. R., Corpus, J. H., & Iyengar, S. S. (2005). Intrinsic and extrinsic motivation orientations in the classroom: Age differences and academic correlates. *Journal of Educational Psychology*, 97, 184–196. DOI: 10.1037/0022-0663.97.2.184

6 Gardner, H. (2004). *The Unschooled Mind: How Children Think and How Schools Should Teach (Tenth anniversary ed.)*. New York: Basic Books.

And the epidemic of disengagement isn't limited to students. Adults are also infected. Even teachers report disengagement at the same levels as the overall US workforce—about 70 percent. Despite the huge numbers of passionate, idealistic teachers entering the field each year, nearly a fifth fail to last even five years. Of those who remain, almost three-quarters are disengaged from their work—the work of molding our children.

You might wonder why we believe that disengagement is more important to talk about than funding, equity, or any of the other topics that dominate media coverage of education. Exploring the causes of disengagement gets at a root issue, one that must be addressed in order for any other improvements to have sustainable impacts. This is not to claim that other issues are unimportant, only that addressing disengagement is a necessary foundation for creating meaningful improvements that will not be undermined by the next change in the political winds.

It's no coincidence that both students and teachers are impacted by the epidemic of disengagement. At heart, both teaching and learning are inherently creative endeavors, and they're both susceptible to the same psychological pitfalls. Moreover, there's evidence that engagement is contagious—and so is disengagement. An engaged teacher is more likely to stimulate engagement in his or her students, and engaged students help a teacher to maintain his or her own engagement. Unfortunately, the same is true of disengagement.

Right now, disengagement is in the lead. If we want schools that provide a better educational experience, we need to understand why so many of the people involved in the learning process fall prey to some form of disengagement. We can gain some understanding by observing engaged students and teachers. It's worth considering school environments where the "inevitability" of disengagement does not exist and engagement is the norm. This turns out to be a difficult challenge since it requires us to get out of the mainstream, which serves well over 90 percent of all students. It is only since 2009 that we have scientifically credible evidence that a different pattern is even possible.

CHAPTER 2

Immunity

• • •

THERE ARE SCHOOLS THAT MANAGE to avoid student disengagement, and if we're interested in truly effective education, it's worth investigating how they do that.

Consider the following two schools, both based in or near Portland, Oregon. The first is the Village Home Education Resource Center, which provides classes to homeschooling families, operating like a community college for students in prekindergarten through high school. Village Home is aimed at family-directed education: in other words, it provides classes and resources, but expects families to be actively engaged in managing the education of each student. Students can choose to take as many or as few classes as they like, and age restrictions are broad and flexible, with students encouraged to take classes based on their interests and abilities. Classes run the gamut, from highly structured classes in math, science, and literature, to a variety of more off-the-wall courses such as embroidery or wilderness skills. Some classes are taught by parents, but most are taught by professional teachers who have often come from the public-education system.

Village Home uses no grading and no standardized curriculum, in order to avoid competition and comparison among students. Each class identifies up front whether homework is required, optional, or nonexistent, and students can further choose the level of intensity of a teacher's feedback. For example, for an essay to be rigorously evaluated with every misspelling or missing comma noted, a student will specifically ask for "hard" feedback.

In contrast, the similarly named but completely unrelated Village Free School (VFS) is a democratic school, where everyone—from the youngest student to the most senior member of the staff—has an identical vote in the running of the school (certain legal and safety issues aside). Three foundational rules have been in place since the school was founded: take care of yourself and other people; take care of the things the school and other people own; and remember that your freedom ends where someone else's begins. Students divide roughly into three groups based on age and inclination, but the boundaries between those groups are porous, and students spend much of their time interacting in mixed-age groups. Classes (or "offerings" in VFS terminology) can be created by any staff or student, are often collaborations, and are always optional. Classes for the oldest students may follow a formal class model, but those for younger students rarely do. Daily rhythms are invented by the community and can be voted out or changed at any time.

The school day has evolved significantly since VFS's inception, and it continues to change. As of this writing, the youngest group of students engages mostly in free play, although they're welcome to join in on offerings and field trips as they like. The middle group of students adheres to mornings spent in "Project Time." Project Time is a student invention where every kid is required to be working on something—the specific project they choose is up to them—and adults are available to assist them. The oldest group has tried out a variety of formats over the years, and recently they put together a more defined curriculum of life skills and academic classes.

You might imagine that neither of these schools could prepare young people for the real world. Yet many graduates from both schools have gone on to college and done very well in that setting. Other graduates have plunged straight into working in fields they found interesting and challenging. Most important for our discussion is the fact that these two schools are based on very different models of education, yet share an interesting common trait: in both schools, disengagement is almost unheard of.[7]

---

7 Berg, D. A., & Corpus, J. H. (2013). Enthusiastic students: A study of motivation in two alternatives to mandatory instruction. *Other Education*, 2 (2), 42–66.

The epidemic of disengagement is nearly ubiquitous in the mainstream education system, regardless of whether schools are public, private, or charter. How do Village Home and VFS manage to avoid this epidemic?

To answer this question, an analogy may be helpful. Let's take a brief detour to London of more than a century ago.

THE WRONG PARADIGM

Mainstream education today is in the same position as medicine was in the mid-1800s: it's based on the wrong model. In 1848, London passed the "Nuisances Removal and Contagious Disease Prevention Act," legislation aimed at getting rid of the noxious materials (including large amounts of raw human sewage) fouling London's streets. The act authorized a large-scale project, which would get that waste out of sight and out of mind, sending it into the storm-water system, an underground system of pipes. Those pipes eventually dumped their contents into the river Thames, which lay at the heart of the city and provided, among other things, the drinking water for two-thirds of the city's residents.

Any modern person, raised with the concept of germ theory, knows that this is a terrible idea. But policy makers of the day were not working under the model of germ theory. The dominant paradigm of disease was miasma theory, which held that bad smells (miasma) directly caused disease. Under this model, getting all that filth off the streets was vitally important; where it went was irrelevant. The 1848 legislation can be viewed as a large-scale endorsement of miasma theory. After a great deal of work and a huge public investment, London's streets were much cleaner and the city's smell was improved—but epidemics of cholera subsequently killed tens of thousands more people.[8]

Miasma theory was not just a single idea. It was the central defining feature of a whole suite of concepts that provided explanations for both

---

8 This is not to imply that cholera would have been otherwise absent; Steven Berlin Johnson reports in his book *The Ghost Map* that given the death tolls before and after the legislated project's completion, it is reasonable to conclude that tens of thousands *more* people died than might have done had germ theory guided policy decisions.

health and disease. Those concepts in turn led to a variety of medical treatments, such as bloodletting and purging (inducing vomiting, sweating, and evacuation of the bowels) that were widely used to treat disease. Miasma theory is intuitively logical—after all, having bad-smelling things like feces and carrion around *did* often correlate with disease, and some people subjected to the common treatments got better. It also had generations of tradition behind it. For experts and lay people alike, it was a paradigm that shaped everyday thinking about health and disease for centuries.

And it was quite simply wrong.

Education today is in a similar state as medicine was when the Thames delivered death to London's residents. The dominant paradigm driving educational legislation today is the delivery model, and it remains firmly rooted in our educational policies despite the impressive quantity and variety of research undermining it. *Simply put, the delivery model considers the core of education to be delivering information from a teacher's head into a student's head.* How well that task has been accomplished is measured by testing the students afterward.

Howard Gardner, a professor of Cognition and Education at the Harvard Graduate School of Education, summed it up this way: "You go to school, a smart person tells you something, and you are expected to learn it and remember it, and if you don't, you are stupid." He went on to say that "rarely is there any conception of learning as a long process of (children's) experimentation, reflection, and self-improvement." He also noted that many people continue to entertain the mistaken delivery notion even after reaching adulthood.[9]

Policy makers working under the delivery model quite logically reason that accounting for information delivery is what really matters in education. It makes sense to standardize all the information and break it down into small chunks, so that as each chunk is delivered, it can be checked off the list, like a FedEx driver marking off his packages. Teachers, who

---

9 Gardner, H. (2004). *The Unschooled Mind: How Children Think and How Schools Should Teach (Tenth anniversary ed.).* New York: Basic Books. p. 102.

are the active elements in this model, are "graded" based on how effective their package delivery was (i.e., how much content is now in each student's head). The very concept of "teacher-proof curricula" inherently assumes that teachers simply need to deliver the content correctly in order for optimal learning to occur. The intuitive logic of the delivery model is compelling—after all, students must be exposed to information in order to learn it—and has resulted in what seems to be complete political consensus that improving schools requires only standardized tests and standardized curricula. Hundreds of billions of dollars in public investment in the United States have endorsed this theory of education in the form of both state and federal legislation that mandate standardized testing and make funding contingent on checking off all the right boxes.

According to renowned global-education scholar Yong Zhao,[10] the Chinese mastered this idea thousands of years ago with horrible long-term consequences for their nation. Now they are doing everything they can to get their systems away from the curses of high-stakes testing and universal standardization. Due to the fact that they do not have a viable replacement paradigm for learning, the Chinese have been struggling with little success for over a decade to bring about meaningful change. They are in a mighty fight against what is for most people the obvious truth about learning.

In fact, although you may not have heard it described in such straightforward terms, the delivery model may seem reasonable to you. It may even sound like common sense. You may, depending on your own experiences, have the uneasy feeling that perhaps it isn't the whole story. If you're a parent, for example, you may have noticed that young children don't seem to work this way. If you're a teacher, you probably know it isn't remotely correct, but more on that later. Once out of school, you may have even noticed that *you* don't work this way. But generations of Americans (and Chinese) have gone through the public-education system and have

---

10 Zhao, Y. (2009). *Catching Up, or, Leading the Way: American Education in the Age of Globalization*. Alexandria, VA: Association for Supervision and Curriculum Development.

learned (though never explicitly been taught) that this is how things work. Teachers impart knowledge, students parrot it back, and that, in a nutshell, is learning.

Unfortunately, this delivery model is wrong. And like miasma theory, policies based on it are doing more harm than good. In particular, this delivery model encourages policies that directly work against some of our primary human needs.

What Are Primary Human Needs?

There are certain things every human needs in order to function well. We need air, food, and water; we need shelter from the elements; and we need sleep. These five examples of primary human needs are commonly understood, and the school system generally recognizes their impact on learning. Subsidized lunch programs attempt to make certain that every student has enough to eat, for example. And kids and their parents are urged to make sure the kids are getting enough sleep, so they can be ready for their day.

But there are three other primary human needs that are well understood in psychological circles, but are only beginning to drift into general public awareness: autonomy, competence, and relatedness. In this book, we refer to supporting another person's primary human needs as *nurturing*—not in a general warm and fuzzy way, but as a psychologically specific term.

Autonomy is exactly what it sounds like: feeling as though we engage in activities of our own volition. In Western societies, this is nearly always associated with making choices for ourselves, but it's worth noting that if two people share a strong enough connection (for example, a strong bond of trust between a parent and a child), directions from the person in authority can still support autonomy under the right conditions. None of us, of course, have complete control over our lives; we all abide by rules from a wide variety of sources, ranging from our legal system to social norms. But all of us know the difference between being helpless and feeling that we have some power to affect our lives.

Competence refers to the sense of mastery we experience as we improve our skills. We perform best when we take on tasks that are within our abilities but that still stretch us slightly. If tasks are too hard, we tend to be frustrated; too easy, and we get bored.

Finally, relatedness is our need to feel connected to other people and to feel that they recognize us for who we are. This is not as simple as having people be nice to us; we must feel that we are seen and respected for our authentic selves.

It's tempting to put these into a category other than "needs." We sometimes use phrases that suggest that autonomy, for example, is more of a nice-to-have quality. The phrase "beggars can't be choosers" implies that choice is more of a luxury and perhaps something that must be earned. But cognitive psychological research has overwhelmingly demonstrated the importance of *all* primary human needs. Being deprived of autonomy may not kill you, but all humans react to the loss of any of these primary human needs with anxiety, depression, and other forms of psychological distress. They may also resort to increasingly desperate attempts to reestablish it.

The tie-in to psychological disorders such as depression is particularly worrying. Boston College developmental psychologist Peter Gray has recently written about the research of Jean Twenge that reveals the declining mental health of American school children going back to the 1940s, when appropriate measures were first used.[11] The steady increases in anxiety and depression don't seem to correlate with external threats (e.g., the economic recession or the Cold War). Instead, increasing depression correlates closely with the increase in children's time spent in highly structured, externally imposed activities (including ever greater amounts of school), and the corresponding decrease in free play. In 2014, suicide was the second most common cause of death among middle-school-aged children in the United States.

---

11 Gray, P. (2013). *Free to Learn: Why Unleashing the Instinct to Play Will Make Our Children Happier, More Self-Reliant, and Better Students for Life*. New York: Basic Books.

The Dilemma

Parents are on the horns of the following dilemma: Their parental responsibility in the world today is to find a school that supports the well-being of their children, so that the parents can live a normal adult life while their kids learn how to grow up to be awesome people. But mainstream schools—the primary institutions that are responsible for supplying and organizing child-nurturing people—have a system in place that actively interferes with the ability of the people in schools to do that job.

* Dropouts are alienated from school instead of welcomed into it, so they disengage from it. Their primary human need for relatedness has been thwarted. According to a report issued by the National Center for Education Statistics[12] in 2012, the risk of dropout was the lowest for white kids (at one in twenty-five) and was the highest for Hispanic kids (at about one in eight) with all other racial groups falling somewhere in between for an overall average of about one in twelve.

* Underachievers experience schools as controlling places where they do not have adequate self-expression, so they disengage from the majority of classroom activities. Their primary human need for autonomy has been thwarted. According to the 2009 High School Transcript Study,[13] also from the National Center for Education Statistics, one in four graduates are below curriculum standards.

* Fauxchievers experience schools as arbitrary systems to be gamed. So while they might seem engaged in school, generally they are emotionally disengaged from some or all of their subjects and do an absolute minimum of work to get whatever level of scores or grades they deem necessary. Their primary human need for competence

---

12 National Center for Education Statistics. (2014, January 1). Fast Facts: Drop Out Rates. Retrieved August 3, 2014, from http://nces.ed.gov/fastfacts/display.asp?id=16

13 Nord, C., Roey, S., Perkins, R., Lyons, M., Lemanski, N., Brown, J., & Schuknecht, J. (2011). *The Nation's Report Card: America's High School Graduates (NCES 2011- 462)*. US Department of Education, National Center for Education Statistics. Washington, DC: US Government Printing Office.

has been thwarted. According to Howard Gardner in his 2004 book *The Unschooled Mind*,[14] at least one in two of those who go on to advanced degrees in their field do so by fauxchievement.

No matter how you slice it, there is a significant risk that the school system will cheat your child out of some or all of the education he or she deserves. Children can be cheated in several ways, but the odds of being cheated are good if you stick to typical mainstream schools, regardless of whether the schools they attend are public, private, or charter. And marginalized populations run the highest risks. Economics, tradition, and widespread community support encourage parents to choose mainstream schools. However, when parents are made aware of the risks involved with attending mainstream schools, their instinctive capacity for nurturing might argue exactly the opposite.

Getting an education today in mainstream schools is comparable to surviving disease up until the early twentieth century: you might manage it, but it will be *in spite of* the dominant paradigm, not because of it. The core idea of delivery that guides educational policy today makes it more and more likely that the harms will be delivered more reliably than the benefits.

To be clear, this isn't a recent problem. According to Eric Haas, Gustavo Fischman, and Joe Brewer in their book *Dumb Ideas Won't Create Smart Kids*,[15] there is evidence that the ideas that have informed the design of schools have been fundamentally the same for at least four thousand years. Different cultures at different times have implemented them in a variety of ways, but the core theories have been consistently wrong.

What's changed in recent history (i.e., the last hundred years or more) is the scale on which the delivery model has been implemented. After all, poor sanitation was always a problem for London—but societal changes in

---

14 Gardner, H. (2004). *The Unschooled Mind: How Children Think and How Schools Should Teach (Tenth anniversary ed.)*. New York: Basic Books.

15 Haas, E., Fischman, G., & Brewer, J. (2014). *Dumb Ideas Won't Create Smart Kids: Straight Talk about Bad School Reform, Good Teaching, and Better Learning*. New York and London: Teachers College Press.

the eighteenth and nineteenth centuries began to make it a truly urgent issue. Cholera only started killing Londoners *en masse* in the early 1800s after population density rose dramatically. Similarly, the delivery model has always been wrong, but as long as schools were relatively small and locally controlled, there was opportunity for people to instinctively lessen their ill effects. But as external pressure has mounted on schools—to increasingly centralize school management since the forties, to focus on science and math since the beginning of the Cold War in the late fifties and early sixties, to increasingly standardize all subjects in all grades and to raise test scores since the eighties and nineties—less and less room has been left for people to find creative paths toward learning. At the same time, children have spent more and more of their time in school, increasing its impact on their lives.

CHAPTER 3

The Way Forward

• • •

BUT IF ALL THIS IS true (and there are reams of research behind it), why are we still using an outdated and potentially harmful model?

The truth is—and this should come as no surprise to anyone who's ever worked in a large organization or tried to change a habit—that change is hard. The delivery model is deeply embedded in the laws surrounding education, in the logistical apparatus supporting it (the textbooks, testing companies, and administrative support structures), and in the mentality of much of the population—even those who theoretically know better. Every time a politician (or parent) worries about test scores, and every time a parent takes a teacher to task for their kids' grades and the impact that may have on their future, the delivery model is in the background. People rarely confront it directly, but it informs their expectations of the system. Moreover, the negative effects of the delivery model appear slowly, over time, and the connection between the delivery model and its negative effects aren't necessarily obvious to a society in which primary human needs are only vaguely understood.

Returning to miasma theory for a moment, it's important to understand that at the point London diverted its sewage into the Thames, preliminary research had already been done that pointed to the notion of invisible infectious agents leading to disease. This research was dismissed by most, often with prejudice. A particularly dramatic example is that of Ignaz Semmelweiss. In the early 1840s, by the careful collection and analysis of empirical data, he developed a successful method for reducing the deaths of his patients, mothers who had just given birth. His method? He required the medical students he was teaching, who had just come from the morgue, to wash their hands before attending maternity patients. This method reduced infections of "puerperal fever" and subsequent deaths by more than half. Despite his thoroughly scientific method and the dramatic practical evidence that he was in fact saving the lives of his patients, he was both professionally and personally ridiculed, and his method was generally rejected until long after his death in 1865.[16]

Letting go of the delivery model is just as difficult for parents and teachers today as letting go of the miasma theory was for physicians over a century ago. Jessica Lahey acknowledges that difficulty when she describes her efforts to explain the seeming paradox of intrinsic motivation to the caring, involved parents of her students. "The less we push our kids toward educational success, the more they will learn," she writes. "The less we use external, or extrinsic, rewards on our children, the more they will engage in their education for the sake and love of learning."[17]

This can feel counterintuitive and frightening. As Alfie Kohn writes in *Punished by Rewards*,[18] "We define ourselves by numbers—take-home pay and cholesterol counts, percentiles (how much does your baby weigh?), and standardized test scores (how much does your child know?). By contrast, we are uneasy with intangibles and...abstractions such as a sense of well-being or an intrinsic motivation to learn." In a sense, we have little experience of grappling with the world in this way; how can we be certain we're doing the right things to help our kids succeed?

At the institutional level, the delivery model has actively suppressed school practices that effectively put the primary human needs for relatedness and autonomy at the center of their educational communities. In one example, Andy Hargreaves and Michael Fullan describe how Grange Secondary School in Northern England had been identified as struggling in 1996, but by 2006 they had made substantially positive reforms by

16 Wootton, David. (2006). *Bad Medicine*. London: Oxford University Press. pp. 215–217.
17 Lahey, Jessica. (2015). *The Gift of Failure*. New York: HarperCollins. p. 22.
18 Kohn, Alfie. (1999). *Punished by Rewards*. New York: Houghton Mifflin Company. p. 10.

supporting their primary population of at-risk, poor immigrant children to have more artistic opportunities. They transformed the entire school into an integrated arts program. After that change was fully implemented, the children were feeling pride in their school and the teachers felt that the new curriculum was dialed into their students' needs. While among the poorest 1 percent of the nation, the school was in the top 2 percent in growth measures of improvement. The school went from 15 percent of students meeting examination standards in 1996 to over 70 percent passing in 2008. The reforms were destroyed in May 2008 when policy decisions above the school-level arbitrarily changed the measures of what counted as success.[19] The school was closed in 2010 and replaced by an academy[20] (the UK equivalent of a charter school). The destructive decisions made "sense" within the context of the delivery model because policy makers insisted on imposing the same standards of performance across all schools, but the decisions were clearly counterproductive to a school community that had found creative ways to address the real needs of its students.

In mainstream schools, teachers are required to operate in an environment that systematically thwarts, or at least neglects, children's primary human needs. And it often thwarts their developmental needs as well, as James P. Comer, founder of the Yale School Development Program, has observed.[21] For decades, the Yale School Development Program has been getting substantive results by focusing primarily on relationships,[22] but over the decades, they came to recognize that their results could be undermined or destroyed by policies and politicking at the district or higher levels just like in the UK example noted above. If we care about equity in education, our first priority should be to make sure that all students have reliable access to primary need-supportive schools. Our second priority

19 Hargreaves, A., & Fullan, M. (2012). *Professional Capital: Transforming Teaching in Every School* (pp. 10–23). New York: Teachers College Press.

20 Hargreaves, A., & Harris, A. (2015). High performance leadership in unusually challenging educational circumstances. Eesti Haridusteaduste Ajakiri. *Estonian Journal of Education*, 3 (1), 28. DOI: 10.12697/eha.2015.3.1.02b

21 Comer, J. P. (2009). *What I Learned in School: Reflections on Race, Child Development, and School Reform*. San Francisco: Jossey-Bass.

22 Ibid..

should be meeting the developmental needs of the children, which the Yale School Development Program has for decades demonstrated to be an effective element of reform.

Why Personal Convictions Are Not Enough

In the case of medicine in the 1800s, most medical practitioners subscribed to miasma theory. The great irony is that, in education today, most teachers are painfully aware of the delivery model's shortcomings. Most teachers, if the model is explicitly described to them, will tell you immediately that of course learning doesn't work that way. Although a thorough discussion of learning is beyond the scope of this book,[23] a useful way to think of it is in terms of growing mental maps. People (of all ages) continually add information to their brain maps, sometimes shifting their perspectives profoundly, sometimes only filling in details—but this can only happen when information is truly integrated, not just cursorily memorized. *Note that in this model, the learner is the active agent.* This comes as no surprise to teachers, who know perfectly well that it's precisely the self-directed students, the ones who take control of their own education, who not only master the material but inspire the teacher to be better.

But teachers have limited control over their own practice; they're heavily constrained by the policies of the multilayered bureaucracy above them. There is no sustainable way for individual teachers, by themselves, to take on the responsibility for maintaining the well-being of their students. Effective teaching is not a solo performance; it requires an ensemble, a whole orchestra, in fact. Everyone—teachers, school administrators, specialists, school psychologists, district administrators, consultants, secretaries, parents, policy makers, and so on—has to play his or her part. A teacher may be devoted to the idea of maintaining his or her students' well-being, but if his or her own needs are going unsupported, he or she is unlikely to be able to sustain that for long.

---

23 For more information, see Berg's website: Schools-of-Conscience.org.

Some teachers manage against the odds to carve out primary human need-supportive spaces. But they do this in the face of an abundance of policies, and an even greater abundance of implicit assumptions and practices in the school system that actively undermine their needs and the practices that support their students. To put it another way, there is a pervasive hidden curriculum working against our school system supporting the well-being of the students and staff.

Any alternative to the current system, such as the schools described earlier, feels unfamiliar and can be mired in a swamp of misinformation. People imagine that supporting autonomy, for example, means feral students or children left entirely to their own devices. But this is equivalent to saying that a workplace can't support autonomy without letting its employees run wild. Daniel H. Pink showed in his best-selling book *Drive* that isn't remotely true. In fact, Pink's account of workplaces such as Google and 3M suggests that in primary need-supportive workplaces, workers actively and enthusiastically engage with the most challenging aspects of the business. Rather than wildness, autonomy-supportive organizations get disciplined enthusiasm when they effectively communicate the nature of their business to their workers.

Perhaps the most seductive appeal of the delivery system is that it seems easy to do. The current, highly standardized model of education may be ineffective and, in fact, downright harmful, but it's relatively simple to describe and implement. It takes far more time, thought, and effort to engage with people in ways that support their primary human needs, particularly if the concept is unfamiliar. It's also much harder for politicians to put together sweeping, get-results-quick programs that take primary human needs into account.

Hope All around Us

At this point, you may be thinking that we're falling inexorably down a gravity well and being sucked into a black hole of educational doom. So it may surprise you to know that we consider exactly the opposite to be true.

Yes, the modern educational system is based on a fundamentally incorrect model, and yes, change is hard. But change *is* possible, especially where we're genuinely motivated, and few things motivate us more strongly than the well-being of our children. And there are signs of hope all around us when we know where and how to look for it.

In the last chapter, we focused on two particular schools in order to discuss the concept of primary human-need support in education. But these are the tip of the iceberg. There are hundreds of schools, using a wide variety of methods and approaches, but all incorporating support for primary human needs—sometimes explicitly, but more often instinctively.[24] Within the public-education system itself there are programs and teachers who manage to push back the dominant paradigm and create a small oasis of autonomy, competence, and relatedness. Think of a teacher who inspired you, who made a subject come alive for you, who gave you confidence in your own abilities and worth—chances are that teacher was instinctively supporting your primary needs.

There is every reason to believe that most teachers want to do better by their students than they are currently allowed to; they would support their students' primary needs if they were supported to do so. There are nurturing classrooms and schools all around us, showing us different approaches to the educational process. And we're in a fantastic position at this point in history—we can take advantage of a body of research on learning and education that is extensive, well-supported, and has stood up through decades of testing. *There is hope all around us.*

So how do we move forward?

---

24 One example: the Yale School Development Program (SDP) has been demonstrating for over forty years that supporting the well-being of children within the school environment is a vital part of successful reform efforts, especially for schools that serve a high proportion of students from marginalized populations. The SDP has focused on three things: pervasively building positive relationships throughout school communities (e.g., relatedness), ensuring that the developmental needs of children inform school decision-making, and viewing schools as complex systems rather than just a relatively simple accumulation of individual interactions.

The Next Steps

Systemic change of our educational system is a topic too large for this book and will need to wait for another—which Berg is working on.[25] But there are things we can do right now to make our students' lives better and to pave the way for deeper change.

Before we get to them, let's take a moment to acknowledge certain things that *won't* solve our problems. Contrary to much of the political rhetoric around education, there are no silver bullets. We cannot simply be more committed to education, let the free market take care of things, enshrine parental choice, or pour more money into a dysfunctional system and hope that everything will work out. Nor could we simply try to clone a primary need–supportive school that already exists (even if everyone could agree on which school to replicate, which seems unlikely). Like most problems in the real world, solving this one will require work, ingenuity, and intelligence.

But there are two early steps that will both help students right now and lay some groundwork for further changes. The first is to start measuring how well schools support primary human needs—in other words, how well they nurture their students.

Effective and efficient learning relies on well-being. As long as well-being is routinely compromised, then learning is also compromised. Simply measuring support for primary human needs may seem insufficient, but there's good reason to believe that it's a necessary first step. As a society we are already oriented toward measurements and tend to focus on problems and solutions that can be framed in terms of data. If we care about primary human needs (and copious research tells us that we should), measuring how well they're supported in school environments is a crucial first step to increasing that support.

Note that we are not claiming that this is an all-encompassing educational theory. There are many discussions about education that need to happen, focusing on teacher training, curriculum development,

---

25 Preliminary work on his next book can be found on Don's website: Schools-of-Conscience.org.

support structures, and a host of other specific facets of the educational system. It's difficult to decide which should be given attention and which should be ignored, and we don't have an easy answer to that. What we are suggesting is a starting point: primary-need support—as measured by the psychological well-being of the children being served by schools—is a necessary foundation upon which any successful educational model must be built. We already recognize that arguing over specific techniques or curricula is pointless when a child arrives at school every day distracted by hunger. If children are struggling to have any of their primary human needs met in school, excellent teaching of a great curriculum is pointless.

Fortunately, tools already exist to help with this measurement. The simplest is perhaps the Gallup Student Poll,[26] which is freely available and essentially just asks people whether they feel engaged. A better instrument is the Hope Survey,[27] which has the advantage of having been validated through peer-reviewed scientific research. The Hope Survey is known as a measure of "school climate," which is one of the areas of measurement that the new federal education legislation (Every Student Succeeds Act) counts as a key school-performance metric. Any school committed to supporting its students can begin measuring their psychological well-being immediately.

Second, each of us has the capacity to nurture the children in our own lives and help to safeguard their engagement—in school and, more importantly, in life. Often we do this instinctively, but we needn't rely on instinct. Psychological research has provided frameworks we can use to help us support primary human needs.

26 Gallup, Inc. (n.d.). Gallup Student Poll. Retrieved June 14, 2017, from http://www.gallupstudentpoll.com/

27 EdVisions. (n.d.). Student Motivation. Retrieved June 14, 2017, from https://www.hopesurvey.org/

In-depth courses and guides to aid in nurturing behavior are available on Berg's website, Schools-of-Conscience.org, but a brief summary is given here. To start with, we can learn to recognize engagement, or the lack thereof. Simply asking children about how engaged they are may or may not be useful; it isn't difficult for children to realize that we'd prefer a particular answer to that question. But engagement can be reliably recognized by external signs such as the following:

How to Recognize Engagement during an Activity[28]

Emotional Engagement

- Presence of task-facilitating emotions (e.g., interest, curiosity, and enthusiasm)
- Absence of task-withdrawing emotions (e.g., distress, anger, frustration, anxiety, and fear)

Behavioral Engagement

- On-task attention and concentration
- High effort
- High task persistence

Cognitive Engagement

- Use of sophisticated, deep, and personalized learning strategies (e.g., elaboration)
- Seeking conceptual understanding rather than surface knowledge (mastery versus performance orientation)
- Use of self-regulatory strategies (e.g., planning)

---

28 Reeve, J. (2012). A Self-Determination Theory Perspective on Student Engagement. In S. L. Christenson et al. (eds.), *Handbook of Research on Student Engagement* (pp. 149–172). New York: Springer. DOI: 10.1007/978-1-4614-2018-7_7

Agentic Engagement

* Proactive, intentional, and constructive contribution into the flow of the activity (e.g., offering input, making suggestions)
* Enriching the activity, rather than passively receiving it as a given

A more poetic expression of noticing engagement is "measuring the light in their eyes." Parents tend to instinctively understand the importance of that light, but can feel that the world tells them to disregard it—to worry instead about performance metrics such as grades and test scores. But that spark of engagement is crucially important not only to a child's prospects in life, but to his or her well-being. As a parent once advised Berg: "The success of a school is indicated by the light in the eyes of its students." If the light in your child's eyes begins to dim, investigate what's going on and consider tweaking the school situation. If it goes out, get your child out of that school. Do everything you can to keep the light in your child's eyes shining bright.

There are specific behaviors that can help to support each of the three primary human needs we've been discussing. The best teachers often instinctively adopt many or all of these behaviors. Although the table below is geared toward a teaching environment, any person interacting with children can benefit from keeping the core principles in mind.

Nurturing Behaviors[29]
Supporting Competence
Do

* Supply activities with optimal levels of challenge
* Use flexible activities that address the same content but can have different levels of challenge
* Give students choices so that they can find appropriately challenging tasks

---

29 Sources:
Ross, D., & Bergin, D. (2011). Recommendations from Self-Determination Theory for Enhancing Motivation for Mathematics. In D. J. Brahier & W. R. Speer (eds.),

Do NOT

* Use the same task for all students without regard for different levels of challenge
* Reduce levels of challenge by giving too much help too early before students have an opportunity to engage with the task

Supporting Relatedness

Do

* Establish norms early that support positive interactions in the classroom
* Show genuine interest in students
* Be well prepared and hold high expectations
* Respond to students and offer choice
* Work to repair damaged relationships

Do NOT

* Use coercive discipline
* Criticize students
* Ignore or give only minimal response to students

Supporting Autonomy

Do

* Offer encouraging informational feedback
* Give meaningful rationales for mandatory tasks
* Acknowledge students' perspectives
* Give several choices
* Listen and respond to students

Motivation and Disposition: Pathways to Learning Mathematics (pp. 55–68). Reston, VA: National Council of Teachers of Mathematics.

Reeve, J. (2009). Why teachers adopt a controlling motivating style toward students and how they can become more autonomy supportive. *Educational Psychologist*, 44 (3), 159–175. DOI: 10.1080/00461520903028990

Do NOT

- Use controlling language, rigid deadlines, and rewards
- Prevent students from handling materials
- Prematurely give solutions
- Require students to work at a rigid pace
- Accept only certain views

CHAPTER 4

The Larger Task

• • •

IDEALLY, WE SHOULD MAKE SYSTEMIC changes to our educational system so that every child's engagement is supported. Remodeling the educational system is a daunting task, one that Berg will explore in detail in his next book. For now, it's worth pointing out that we should take a principled approach instead of a prescriptive one. In other words, while it may be tempting to lay down detailed instructions on how to change existing schools, that's precisely what we *shouldn't* do. Such a top-down, controlling approach would be a good way to thwart the primary psychological needs of those on the receiving end of the prescriptions. A properly principled approach, on the other hand, provides guidance without dictating specifics and requires the kind of involvement that is most likely to support the needs of those directly affected by change.

The most important litmus test of positive changes is to see improvement in the well-being of the children and teachers at the center of the system (and eventually all the humans involved). Well-being should not be the only measured outcome, but it should be given the highest priority.

As examples all around us show, schools can be supportive environments and people can maintain their intrinsic motivation through their schooling. Our job now is to ensure that every child, regardless of circumstances, has the chance to experience such a school.

Therein lies a new challenge. How do we find the schools we want our children to attend? Surprisingly, there is no publicly available comprehensive list of schools, let alone a list gathered by a neutral organization that neither has a stake in running a school nor selling something to parents for a profit. State governments that are legally responsible for public schools have listings, and in Oregon at least, the state includes some of the private schools that choose to be listed. But the listings are not comprehensive of all your real options, are often out of date, and are difficult to access, and the listings don't give you any useful information about the uniqueness of each operation. The National Center for Education Statistics surveys private schools[30] every other year, but that data is not made easily available to parents nor does it include *all* of their options.

Berg sits on the board of a local nonprofit that started and ran an alternative to school for teens for a few years. During the planning process, it was surprisingly difficult to get good information about the schools and education options in our area, so that we could identify what gap in services we should fill. That lack of good information contributed to the short life of our initial program.

Berg started Schools of Conscience, a nonprofit organization, to build the nurturing capacity of K–12 schools. The first major project is called ChoosEd. It is an online database that will provide comprehensive up-to-date information on all the K–12 education options available in each area we serve. The big idea is IMDb meets the NEA meets the PTA. IMDb is the Internet Movie Database that is the largest database of movies in the world, and it was started by a movie fan trying to share his passion for movies by collecting information about them. The National Education Association (NEA) is the largest teacher's union in the country. It is a major political force to be reckoned with at both state and national levels. The parent teacher association (PTA) is also a force to be reckoned with in most schools as one of the primary vehicles for parents to communicate with their schools. We want to share our passion for schools by sharing

30 Private School Universe Survey (PSS). (n.d.). Retrieved June 14, 2017, from https://nces.ed.gov/surveys/pss/

information about them, and in the process, we will actively advocate for the well-being of all children in our society.

The pilot project will cover the Portland metropolitan area in Oregon. Next, we will expand to cover the whole state and eventually the nation. The plan is to have a few volunteers at every school, representing parents and staff, who will maintain the accuracy of the listings for each school. Those volunteers will be recruited and trained by one of our staff. We will also use this unique reach into the educational world to convene gatherings that focus on the shared commitment to nurture children to become good citizens. The gatherings will be deliberately diverse in terms of representing both parents and professionals at public, private, charter, and homeschool organizations.

The funding for this project will come from parents, school boards, and other organizations that want to invest in a properly educated citizenry. The basic information in the database will be freely available to all via the website ChoosEd.org. More detailed information will be available to our members. Membership will be an attractive option for school boards that want regular access to customized reports about local and regional trends, advocates and agencies who need deep analysis of the education sector, and those who would like to participate regularly in our gatherings. Ultimately, this project will harness a laser-focused political power devoted exclusively to nurturing our nation's children. Our unwavering moral commitment to the well-being of all children will make it possible for us to transcend partisan politics. We will be uniquely positioned to hear from both families and educators. Our perspective will be informed by real, solid information about schools and the children they serve, independent of political parties, working conditions, profit motives, and who is running the government.

The political movement that will come out of the ChoosEd project will enable K–12 schools to finally apply the unprecedented understanding of how our own minds work and how learning occurs. We encourage you to start by becoming well-informed. You've already taken the first step by finding out about the dilemma you face. Moving forward, we can work together to resolve the dilemma for future parents by providing them with more and better information about schools that can nurture their children, schools that will fit because they keep the light in children's eyes shining bright.

67022905R00024

Made in the USA
San Bernardino, CA
19 January 2018